<u>Also By Emily Matthews:</u>

Resizing Your Life: Time To Move On?

Assisting Your Relatives in the Resizing Process

Copyright © 2025 by Emily Matthews

All rights reserved. No part of this book may be reproduced or used in any manner without written permission of the copyright owner except for the use of quotations in a book review.

All names are fictional. All scenarios are semifictional composites of numerous encounters with people in the ER or in real estate, and do not reflect any single real-life occurrence. Any resemblance to any individual or any individual's experience is purely accidental and unintentional.

First paperback edition July 2025

ISBN 979-8-218-74083-2

Independently Published

Acknowledgments

Naomi B. for all your help in formatting and design.

Table of *Contents*

[1] Is It Time? — 1
Stages of decision-making, Understanding your role

[2] Safety: Don't Neglect the Issue — 9
Falls, Levels of Hoarding, Driving Safety, Medical safety solutions

[3] Procrastination: Not the Best Tactic — 31
Change the unknown to the known, Stop analysis paralysis, Fear of giving up something

[4] Advance Planning: General — 37
POA, Guardians, Estate Planning

[5] Advance Planning: Where to Live — 49
Planning (with family dynamics), Advance planning for making a move, Housing options

[6] Resistance, Resetting, and Reframing — 65
The point of reframing

[7] The Process — 73
Beware Google reviews, Beware pricing unsupported by data, Beware of not having the house ready

[8] Selling the House — 83
Responding to Offers, Accepted Offer, Closing (Sale)

About the Author
Contact Information

Assisting

Your Relatives in the

Resizing Process

CHAPTER ONE

Is It Time?

When as a child I laughed and wept, time crept.
When as a youth I grew more bold, time strolled.
When I became a full-grown man, time ran.
When older still I daily grew, time flew.
(Henry Twells)

Probably everyone over 35 can relate to this verse. The only situation where it doesn't seem to apply is when people are thinking-or *not* thinking-about their living situation and potential future changes to that. Most people

Chapter One – Is It Time?

who are older or who have older relatives, just don't want to consider this.

But when senior parents begin slowing down visibly, often their children (or nieces & nephews) then begin wondering if they should make a move to something better suited to their abilities. The kids may begin to drop hints or even start outright pressuring their parents/relatives to sell and resize into something smaller or more convenient. The younger generation might have good reasons for feeling anxious, but the seniors themselves see no cause for alarm. The family members can find themselves at cross-purposes resulting in a stalemate situation.

The thought of moving away from a well-loved home can send some people into a panic. Others may feel they can't wait to leave because of the burden it has become. Or, if both homeowners are living, one can't wait to leave all the work behind and just rent someplace, while the other one doesn't want to budge. You will never truly know how they feel until you talk to them openly without anything that could be perceived as an "agenda."

Chapter One – Is It Time?

On the flip side, there are times when senior parents *want* to sell and downsize, but their family resists! They may be upset that "the old homestead" will be gone. The big family gatherings won't happen there anymore and they grieve that change. Again, the solution is to have open communication.

The goal is to understand everyone's concerns and to share without making any demands or decisions. Those can come later. At the beginning, just being able to talk is what's important.

Communication: not just words

The most important part of communication is listening. And hearing not simply what is said, but what is *meant*. When people make statements, they often have in mind unspoken concerns. Merely listening to the bare statement doesn't give the full picture. The best way to understand what your parents are thinking is to ask further questions. Consider the following examples:

- "There's so much to do around here"

Chapter One – Is It Time?

- "I'll never leave this house until they take me out in a box"
- "I just can't face the thought of moving"
- "This is too overwhelming"

There are many potential meanings to each statement, and your job is to discover what is really the issue behind each one. Let's explore several different possible meanings.

There's so much to do. This could mean that your older relative wants more help with managing things at home. Or it could mean they're just getting tired of all the maintenance and want an easier living situation. Another possibility is that your mom has had to take on extra duties because of your dad's failing health, and is unaware of resources they could use. It could indicate a deferred-maintenance item that they believe they aren't able to afford.

I'll never leave. This is a dramatic way of making a point. Perhaps you pressured your dad a bit too much and he just wants time to think over the possibilities. Or maybe your mother can't bear to give up a cherished collection

Chapter One – Is It Time?

that she knows she'd have no space for in a new place. Maybe there is a fear that "our kids think we're slipping" and they don't want to face their changing health. This defensive statement always has another meaning, and your job is to uncover what that is.

I can't face moving. This could mean simply feeling overwhelmed at the logistics of packing up a household of 40 years' accumulations. Or they really mean they can't face the fact that "moving" signals (to them) some unwelcome change in status. Your relatives are showing you they haven't moved through the *stages of decision-making* yet.

It's overwhelming. Making a move feels overwhelming to everyone! There's no way around it: moving is always stressful. So what is the specific reason? Is it the thought of researching and finding someplace else? Is it reluctance to part with *stuff*? Or is it a fear of giving up the familiar?

Chapter One – Is It Time?

Stages of decision-making

This is borrowed from healthcare. When someone gets an unwelcome diagnosis, they are observed to move through *stages of feeling or being,* until acceptance is reached. Just so, the *decision to move* goes through these stages also. These stages considered in the context of making a move are:

Denial: "I'm doing just fine here!" "My/his/her mobility isn't *that* bad yet." "My/our finances aren't *that* shaky; the bank wouldn't *really* foreclose!"

Anger: "Why does s/he/they want me to move!? How dare they!" "Why did life treat me/us so badly? We don't want to give this up!" "Interfering relatives!"

Bargaining: "We can probably put off those repairs for a while yet." "We'll just turn down the thermostat if it starts costing too much." "Can't you (i.e. family) just come over and help some more?" "I have plenty of time; I don't really have to move *that* soon."

Chapter One – Is It Time?

Depression: This can take many forms, but really seems to be very fleeting in the case of planning a needed move. Some people skip right over this stage.

Acceptance: This is the stage when people start actively looking at alternative living arrangements. This is the fun stage! There really are a lot of opportunities for any budget.

Understanding your role

There's a quote attributed to Mark Twain that says, "When I was a boy of fourteen, my father was so ignorant I could hardly stand to have the old man around. But when I got to be twenty-one, I was astonished at how much he had learned in seven years." Even though he didn't really say it, it illustrates how the process of time can alter parent-child relationships.

This principle of changing roles is something nobody consciously thinks of. Rather, people simply *act* in certain ways. Unconsciously, roles start to shift as both parents and their children age. The children may ask the

Chapter One – Is It Time?

parent's help or advice when they become parents themselves. Then by the time the grandkids are teens, their grandparents may start asking them or their parents for help. Nobody thinks much about it.

But when it comes to decisions closely impacting their whole lives as they know it, seniors may shut down. They may say things like, "I didn't tell you what career to follow; I let *you* choose," or "Stop interfering! It's *my* life." The adult children could actually know more about types of apartments, condos, or assisted living, but when they try to inform their parents, it turns into a heated discussion.

Remember that your senior parents still have lived through experiences you haven't yet had. They will need time to go through the *stages of decision-making*. It could help to ask them to go through a "pro and con" exercise. They should write down and save lists of the pros and cons of resizing each week for two months, *without reading the previous lists*. After that time, get all the lists out and read them. Certain themes will appear that can help clarify everyone's thinking, and get a meaningful discussion started.

CHAPTER TWO

Safety: Don't Neglect the Issue

When people are considering their options, usually preferences, emotions, and opinions take precedence over safety. Is the situation safe?

But safety is too underrated. To illustrate, considering the EMS response, the staff involved are always reminded to consider safety first. "Is the scene safe?" is the first question we are trained to ask, because otherwise, we might just jump in to help and become casualties ourselves.

During disaster-training simulations we'd have to ensure that "contaminated" patients were deconned

Chapter Two – Safety: Don't Neglect the Issue

(decontaminated) first before providing care. One or two dedicated staff in PPE would be in charge of that; then the deconned patients were handed over into the safe zone for further care by the staff in that zone.

This principle applies to home situations also. There is definitely an illusion of safety that can keep some people in their homes for too long. But… is the situation safe? They may be unable to keep up with chores, so the place gets more cluttered, resulting in trip hazards. Or they become physically weak, leading to increased risk of falls. Often when people procrastinate making a move, there is real danger.

They may not *be* safe, but *feel* safe. Be patient while you explain that at the very least, they should get a medical alert device if they are in danger of falling. This can buy them time to sort through their feelings about making a move. It can help to point out that this may mean they won't risk being found on the floor after being there for days…but be as tactful as possible when you have the conversation.

Chapter Two – Safety: Don't Neglect the Issue

> Many times in ER, there would be calls on the scanner "found on floor, unknown time." They'd tripped or fallen in their "safe" home, and were unable to get up. Obviously, those people had waited too long to move into safer quarters, and would arrive hypothermic, injured, and usually unconscious.
>
> Upon discharge they were usually given nursing home placement at whatever facility could take them. Maybe some of them were only there for rehab but I'm sure some of them never ended up in their "safe" homes again, especially if their injuries meant they couldn't get about anymore. They had procrastinated until decisions were no longer theirs to make.

    The national Council on Aging has a home safety checklist that can be downloaded at this site: https://www.ncoa.org/adviser/sleep/home-safety-older-adults/ There is another resource that has pictorial representations of common hazards: the HSSAT, or Home Safety Self-Assessment Tool. There are several sites where you can obtain this tool, and the drawings at the

Chapter Two – Safety: Don't Neglect the Issue

end of the book illustrates the types of safety hazards that are featured in the HSSAT.

Falls

The causes of falls are numerous. If falls have become frequent, a doctor should be consulted. Falls don't necessarily mean a person has to relocate. That will depend on the *cause* of the falls. I.e. maybe the person needs a pacemaker. Maybe they need their meds to be adjusted. Sometimes once the cause is corrected, there is no need to consider immediate relocation.

Chapter Two – Safety: Don't Neglect the Issue

> Anita arrived by ambulance because of a fall. (Fortunately, she had a medical alert bracelet). She'd had no symptomatic precursors to a fall, such as tripping, feeling dizzy, unwell, etc. She expressed that she'd "have to leave her home because of the falls."
>
> As we spoke, she became unconscious. The monitor showed her pacemaker was malfunctioning. Almost as soon as she'd lost consciousness, she awoke again, because the pacer started up again. She said, "See? This is happening more and more. I'll have to leave my home." But once her pacemaker was fixed, she was able to live at home safely.

Besides the HSSAT checklists, there are three specific safety situations that should be acknowledged even though most people don't like talking about them. The first is **hoarding**. The second is **driving safety**, and the third is **medical safety**.

Levels of hoarding

In healthcare, there are scales and tools for just about anything. For example, there's a scale for scoring

Chapter Two – Safety: Don't Neglect the Issue

pressure sores. Or the Elderly Mobility Scale. There are no scales to measure hoarding so I will call them levels one, two, and three.

Level one hoarders are collectors. They have collections they can't bear to part with and usually have all kinds of display cabinets to house the collections, although sometimes they just keep everything in drawers and cabinets. I've sold several homes with so many cabinets it was difficult to walk through the place. Even the kitchens would have cabinets crammed in available spaces. One person had an entire room (the biggest in the house) devoted to the collection, which was housed on multiple tables with about 2 feet of space between them, plus items in display cabinets lining the walls.

At times, the collection might involve cars or tools. One home sale I facilitated had a 6-car shed, and all those cars had to be rehomed. Many older homes have sheds or workrooms in the basement that are *filled* with tools, usually in neat arrangements.

Level one hoarders might agree to use an estate sale to liquidate the collections, or they might decide to give

Chapter Two – Safety: Don't Neglect the Issue

away the treasures to family or friends who appreciate them. Collections can be more *or* less valuable than people suspect, so it pays to have an estate sale company or appraiser come in to give an idea of the value.

Even if there are no plans yet to make a move, getting rid of *stuff* can make the place safer. Disposing of the items when everyone can talk things over can prevent future family squabbles. And it can allow seniors to continue living in their homes without the hazards associated with just having too many things around. A good resource to help with dividing collections is www.fairsplit.com Further suggestions about collections are in Resizing Your Life: Time to Move On?

Level two hoarders don't have collections; rather they just don't get rid of anything. They may have boxes filling the basement, spare room, or attic. Furniture like sideboards, cabinets, and desks are stuffed with miscellaneous things, some valuable, some junky. There might be piles of books or magazines on tables. But there is room to walk, and all the stuff is packed away after a fashion.

Chapter Two – Safety: Don't Neglect the Issue

This situation doesn't necessarily present a safety hazard, unless furniture itself is being hoarded. Does anybody really need 13 end tables in their basement? Or eleven couches and loveseats in the living room? I've been in homes that were so jammed with furniture, there were "tunnels" to walk through.

The first step in resizing for level two hoarders is to start sorting through what is worth keeping and what's not. Beware of "maybe" piles, as they can get big in a hurry, resulting in not eliminating anything. This process can be done long before deciding to move and has the benefit of decreasing stress when the actual time comes to transition into a different living situation.

If there is so much furniture it's dangerous, the best way to resolve this is to sell some of it off before there's an accident. You can point out that by decreasing the clutter, it makes them safer and can possibly mean they'll be able to stay safely at home longer.

Chapter Two – Safety: Don't Neglect the Issue

> Elroy's wife couldn't bear to get rid of anything. Their attic was stuffed with cardboard gift boxes and fabric (a fire hazard), and the basement filled with storage bins and furniture. She didn't even know what was in the bins, but demanded the contents should *not* be thrown out. Their living space was crowded with furniture.
>
> When they relocated to a small condo, their family was finally able to get involved and help Elroy get rid of some of the items. His wife still insisted on taking too much furniture, so that was stored in their new basement. Elroy had to wait till she passed on to eliminate all the extra furniture, but at least their new living space was free of clutter (safer) and all the boxes and bins were gone.

Level three hoarders are the ones they make TV shows about. The home is literally filled with junk strewn all over the place. There is no law against living in a dirty place, but when safety is threatened, this environment becomes a problem.

Level three hoarders will need extensive help to be able either to remain in their homes or to sell. Sometimes the house has so many environmental problems it will take

Chapter Two – Safety: Don't Neglect the Issue

more than mere tidying. Of course, having shoes, old food, boxes, clothes, old radios, tools, lightbulbs, bicycle wheels, brooms, and books on almost every surface, including the floor, means there's a huge risk of falling. If the individual resists cleaning up, the county public health services might be able to help.

Other times, the hoarding might involve machines, cars, or tools. These are housed in garages or outbuildings. If the space is too crowded, it quickly becomes unsafe. If a person fell outside, there are the added risks of being harder to find, and being exposed to the elements.

> I showed an estate (probate) home once that had multiple outbuildings where piled-high junk could be seen through the windows. Even the *upper* window of the barn revealed piles of things! None of these buildings was accessible to potential buyers due to safety concerns: the MLS stated "off limits." There was also yellow police tape surrounding an area, so it was safe to assume the person had fallen and had been found somewhere in or around these buildings. Extreme hoarding is dangerous!

Chapter Two – Safety: Don't Neglect the Issue

Driving safety

When I worked in ER, I saw my share of auto crashes. Some were caused by mere carelessness, but too many happened because the driver/s were elderly and at a point in life where their driving was no longer safe. For example, one lady came in via ambulance after she drove her car right into and under a slow-moving semi with flashers on. She was lucky to be alive and had an arm full of glass, among other injuries.

What happens when you know your relative isn't safe driving anymore? It's much safer for them-and their potential victims-for you to try to intervene before the unthinkable happens. You may encounter hurt feelings, outright anger, or possible accusations, but sometimes it's actually very easy to have the dreaded "conversation."

If the situation does turn into an argument, it's best to ask open-ended questions and defer the topic for another time, unless the safety issue is so pressing it can't be ignored. The following illustrations show what happens when unsafe driving is left to continue too long.

Chapter Two – Safety: Don't Neglect the Issue

The airbags:

They both arrived by ambulance. Percy & his friend Eileen had been to visit another friend who lived in a senior complex with an onsite underground parking facility. After saying goodbye to her, they found the car, Percy put it in gear, and…floored it. Right into a concrete pillar.

The impact deployed the airbags, which ended up fracturing Eileen's sternum, because she was wearing a lifeline. The airbag literally punched it into her chest. The police declined to give a citation because the incident happened on private property. If they had, it would've made my job easier because I had to have *the talk* with Percy's family who came to pick him up; he wasn't injured.

I had to ask them if they'd ever had a discussion with his family doctor as to driving. I had to point out that Eileen was hospitalized because of him, "…and what if this had been on the open road? What if he killed someone? Or himself?" They admitted they "had a few concerns" but they weren't prepared for any "confrontation." They were just too worried about taking steps to ensure safety.

Chapter Two – Safety: Don't Neglect the Issue

They left and I genuinely felt dread for what could happen next time.

Inattentive driving:

Barb's mother had never been the most attentive driver even when young. Now, though she was only in her early 60s, her driving ability had markedly deteriorated. Barb, an RN, recognized signs of dementia, but her siblings refused to acknowledge it. Their dad's only response to Barb's concerns was, 'Well, I do most of the driving."

In the meantime, her mom's driving worsened to the point she'd forget where she'd parked at a store, or would be gone for three times as long as it should take to do an errand. When she came home, she'd refuse to answer questions as to why it took her so long, but Barb suspected her mother had actually become lost.

Barb was concerned enough that she called her mom's doctor's office. The gatekeeper immediately tried to hide behind HIPAA, but Barb said, "I'm not *asking* for info, I'm *telling* you something!" She was able to get through to the office staff and explained that her dad

Chapter Two – Safety: Don't Neglect the Issue

would never bring up her mother's failing health and driving ability.

She told them she expected them to fill out the simple form, available from the DMV, that would give a valid picture of her mom's ability to drive. (There is also a non-medical version of this form for "lay people" and law enforcement to use).

Because she was a nurse, Barb knew what to do and avoided being seen as the "family troublemaker" by getting the *doctor* to agree to include this evaluation at the next office visit. However, suddenly her parents decided to sell their home & rent an apartment, even before the next appointment! Once they moved, her dad felt able to put his foot down and forbade Barb's mom to touch the car keys. Her mom never said a word about wanting to keep driving.

The speeder:

Ethel and Joan, best friends, went everywhere together. Ethel had given up driving so Joan took them

Chapter Two – Safety: Don't Neglect the Issue

both everywhere. Joan had finally traded in her ancient Buick for a brand-new model. She'd depended on the grinding noise the old car made when turning the ignition key while running…to *tell* her the engine was running. As you know, cars don't do that (except for ancient ones).

She turned the key…no noise…somehow she got the car into drive without realizing it. When it started rolling, she panicked and hit the brake as hard as she could. Except it wasn't the brake pedal; it was the accelerator! Rocketing over a viaduct at close to 100 mph, she finally skimmed a guard rail which spun the car around and stopped it.

Fortunately no other vehicles were involved. Neither Joan nor Ethel were seriously injured, but they could have ended up in the valley below or in a multi-vehicle crash. Joan was issued a citation and I'm fairly certain her driving days would be over due to un-insurability, if not an inability to pass a driving test. The police may even have filled out the DMV form indicating inability to drive safely. Her car was totaled.

Chapter Two – Safety: Don't Neglect the Issue

County sheriff's report/press release:

"The preliminary investigation indicates that a 2015 Jeep Cherokee Sport, operated by (a) 76-year-old…was traveling **northbound** on Interstate 43 in the **southbound** lanes of travel…a 43-year-old from Sheboygan, was operating a 2018 Volkswagen Golf southbound on Interstate 43 in the southbound lanes of travel. Both vehicles collided head on…Both operators were pronounced dead at the scene of the crash…" Please don't let this be your elderly relatives and their victim!

Medical safety

Something that may escape notice until too late is medical safety. At times, seniors are physically capable of handling various chores but may be forgetful when it comes to taking medications. They may take them inappropriately or forget altogether. Or just refuse to take them. When meds are not taken correctly it presents a medical risk. Imagine taking too many blood thinners or oral hypoglycemics. That could kill someone.

Chapter Two – Safety: Don't Neglect the Issue

It is possible to prevent dangerous med situations by having a doctor evaluate for home health care. Especially if someone is already receiving some home health care, getting a med regime added in shouldn't be too hard. There are automated cylindrical pill dispensers for people to use, that will sound an alarm and open at the correct time. Only the right slot will open. Once a week, staff will come in, unlock it, and fill all the drawers. Having something like this allows medications to be taken at the correct times.

Sometimes meds themselves are dangerous. The newer blood thinners (Eliquis, Pradaxa, Xarelto) are examples. There is no reversal as with coumadin and vitamin K. These can cause hidden bleeding, leading to weakness, which leads to falls. Other meds to watch are blood pressure meds. They can cause the BP (and sometimes heart rate) to drop too low, leading to dizziness and falls. Oral hypoglycemics also are dangerous when taken incorrectly.

Because medications affect people differently as they age, it's wise to have the doctor review them

Chapter Two – Safety: Don't Neglect the Issue

especially if the person has taken them the same way for years. Doses might need to be changed.

> Taking meds incorrectly or without a timely MD review can give an inaccurate picture in the event a person does move to assisted living or gets home health to set up the meds. Pete had been taking oral hypoglycemics for years…when he remembered. (His wife didn't see it as her duty to remind him). Once his wife died, it became apparent that he could no longer stay safely at home, as he was just too forgetful. His family got his healthcare POA activated and moved him into a CBRF.
>
> The care plan included his oral hypoglycemics. For the first time in years, Pete was taking meds as directed, but the dose was in reality too high. He was found unresponsive due to low blood sugar. After a hospital stay, the doctor discontinued the medication. His blood sugar was managed by diet alone after that.

There are various other medical situations that may need reviewing over time. Any progressive illness eventually reaches a point where some type of life

Chapter Two – Safety: Don't Neglect the Issue

alteration becomes inevitable. Medical devices can be implemented or an actual move might be needed.

Medical safety solutions: Assistive devices and retrofitting

If your parents or relatives aren't ready to consider transitioning into a different situation, retrofitting the home or providing assistive devices can buy them enough time to mull their situation over. The most important safety device that all elderly should consider is some sort of emergency call device, in case they do fall. A thorough safety check of the home can be done. Contacting the County ADRC is the best place to begin.

Retrofitting can be done if the layout, condition, and structure of the home permit. Retrofitting makes no sense if a house is deteriorating. If that's the case, it should be sold or repaired before it gets worse.

Retrofitting can include grab bars, toilet risers, ramps, or converting a main-floor space into a laundry room. If a senior is a veteran there are VA grants that may

Chapter Two – Safety: Don't Neglect the Issue

be available to retrofit a home. Contact the local CVSO (County Veterans Service Officer) who can assist.

> Depending on the budget and eligibility, a house can be transformed into a "nursing home" without the expense of a nursing home. When I did home health, I oversaw a care plan for Roger, who was quadriplegic following an accident. He was able to move his arms enough to use a TV remote or eat with special tools.
>
> His ranch home had been altered to provide what he needed right there. There was a Hoyer lift, hospital bed, and wheelchair. The closet of his bedroom had been altered to include a toilet and roll-in shower. Caregivers came five times daily to cook and serve meals, take care of hygiene needs, and put him to bed. He had a bedside alarm for night time emergencies.

Chapter Two – Safety: Don't Neglect the Issue

The above is an extreme example, but it illustrates the fact that it's not *always* necessary to move out of a family home. However, many times deferred maintenance or inability to retrofit does mean a move will be inevitable. It's better to sell a deteriorating house before it gets worse, than to stay in it till it becomes a health hazard.

How transitioning might help/change things

Sometimes all it takes is a change of environment or routine to revamp the situation. If meds are being taken as prescribed for the first time in years, be on the lookout for side effects. If there is a need to declutter or downsize, doing so could mean being able to stay in the current home a bit longer, because the clutter is gone. Or if a move is necessary, decluttering *early* will alleviate stress later when it's actually time to move.

Depending on variables, resizing into a condo, apartment, or other living arrangement might help an unsafe driving situation resolve itself. Sometimes people realize that they can order many goods online, or have a taxi service take them where they need to go, only *after*

Chapter Two – Safety: Don't Neglect the Issue

resizing into a different home. Or the unsafe driver just leaves all driving to the safe one.

If your parents live in town, and they opt to stay in their current home, there are often transportation alternatives more readily available than out in the country. They may surprise you and decide to use these resources, rather than move. If they live outside of a city, resizing might be essential to prevent highway accidents.

If it just won't work to retrofit or pursue home health care, a move into an RCAC might be the solution for someone who needs some assistance but is not completely dependent. RCACs provide separate, self-contained apartments complete with kitchens, but have assistive staff on hand if needed.

The main point is to consider how safety enters into future plans. It's a good idea to start considering safety issues before an unsafe situation develops.

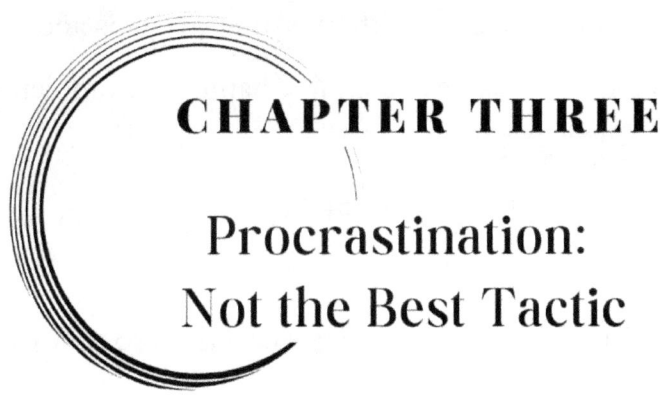

CHAPTER THREE

Procrastination: Not the Best Tactic

We all do it. Some of us rarely, some all the time; it's their lifestyle. It really is a thief! Procrastination serves as a coping mechanism for short-term relief of negative emotions. Stress is a common trigger, but fears also can be. When considering resizing, the most common fears are those of the unknown, of making a mistake, or of having to give up something.

Change the unknown to the known

Have you heard the saying, "Better the devil you know than the devil you don't know?" Fears of the

Chapter Three - Procrastination: Not the Best Tactic

unknown can be dealt with by listing the pros and cons of making a move as described in Chapter 1. Completing this exercise helps people hone in on what *exactly* they don't like about the thought of moving, instead of staying in a vague "I don't like the idea" zone.

In other words, *define* the negatives so they can be acknowledged and worked through. Even though your parents still might not like what is now known, at least it has a description and a name. Facing something definite is always easier than facing the unknown.

The other side of doing the pros and cons is that people might realize that transitioning into a new living situation might actually have some benefits. Or it might convince the hesitant spouse at least to be open to what the ready-to-go one wants.

Stop analysis paralysis

Fears of making the wrong decision can be dealt with by first determining what the concern is. Is it worry about getting rid of the "wrong" things? Is it a concern about being "fair" with distribution of personal items? Or

Chapter Three - Procrastination: Not the Best Tactic

is it a fear that "we might end up living in a place we hate?"

The solutions to these match what the issues are. If there are a lot of personal possessions, sometimes seniors hesitate to toss them because they don't want to get rid of something that might be useful. If family dynamics are such that it's difficult to ask in person, perhaps it will work to send everyone an email about what's there and to ask if they want it.

Chapter Three - Procrastination: Not the Best Tactic

> George had lived in the same place for over 70 years. He'd saved a *lot* of things "because they might be useful." He wanted to sell a tract of land with a storage building on it, but the building was filled with these things. He absolutely refused to toss anything even when none of the relatives said they wanted e.g. the old broken sections of chain-link fence, or any of the other items in there.
>
> The deadline for closing was getting near and the shed was still full! Eventually one set of relatives stepped up and volunteered to take everything, because they had a farm and it was *possible* (not probable) that they'd use the stuff. George was able to let go because he was satisfied that someone *might* be able to use it. (That family actually got rid of almost everything later).

Fears about "ending up in the wrong place" can be alleviated by making some advance plans as described later in Chapter 4. It really does pay to start researching even a couple years ahead of when a move might become unavoidable. Researching should include visiting places in

Chapter Three - Procrastination: Not the Best Tactic

person. Specific questions to ask are covered in <u>Resizing Your Life.</u>

Fear of giving up something: things

I've sold a number of houses that were stuffed with multiples of some sort. Multiple pieces of furniture, dish sets, towels, or holiday decorations; you name it, they had it! A lot of times the owners kept those things, not because they really wanted them, but because they couldn't face having to sort through and give away or donate them. Or because of fears of making a mistake in getting rid of them.

You can help your relatives by going through those boxes with them and hauling it away for them. If there are items that family members *would* want, they can put their names into a drawing or everyone can get together to talk about how to share them out. One useful resource is <u>www.fairsplit.com</u>

When the owners of too much stuff are afraid to give up anything, it pays to remember that communication is the key. If you ask the right questions, the truth will

Chapter Three - Procrastination: Not the Best Tactic

manifest itself as to why they don't want to part with the things. But if you believe they are hoarding due to reduced mental capacity, you should alert medical professionals.

Fear of giving up something: autonomy

The biggest fear of seniors facing declining health or mobility is that of losing autonomy aka fear of being a burden. But procrastinating because of this fear is the worst thing possible and can actually *lead* to loss of autonomy! Because if someone stays in an unsafe situation too long, they could have a mishap that results in not being able to stay there anymore. At that point of crisis, they will not have choices anymore.

If your relatives' situation is unsafe, steps should be taken to minimize safety concerns. The County Aging and Disability Resource Center (ADRC) can provide resources for assistive devices, home care, etc. Keeping the current environment as safe as possible buys time to explore options. They should take as active a part as possible in deciding between different possibilities.

CHAPTER FOUR

Advance Planning: General

Advance planning is something we all know we need to do, and yet we all procrastinate. The need to do so becomes more urgent as time progresses. Especially if someone has never drafted a POA or will before.

What happens if your elderly relative has started to wander and gets lost? Or if they light the stove and forget about it? Observed behaviors like this are alarming. At what point does a family step in and start making decisions *for* the person? These questions are why advance planning needs to be done. There are different documents to deal with this scenario.

Chapter Four – Advance Planning: General

Or what if the elderly senior has a disabled child or sibling…or even spouse? This is another special situation that should be considered, especially if the disabled individual lives with the elderly senior. It doesn't pay to wait until the elderly caregiver is disabled by a stroke, MVA, or other medical crisis, to start deciding about the disabled person they care for.

An estate-planning lawyer can help with setting up a trust, drafting POAs, and any other contingency that needs to be planned for. In many families, this has already been addressed, but sadly there are cases where e.g. an elderly person is found deceased, along with their deceased disabled child that was living with them.

Chapter Four – Advance Planning: General

> Judy arrived at the ER with medical symptoms of a UTI. (UTIs can be relatively minor for younger people, but often elderly patients are devastated from them and have to be admitted). She had a developmentally disabled son, whom her husband was caring for at home.
>
> She offered the information that "they were getting older and starting to think about how to provide for him when they were gone." Since they had procrastinated thus far, I was concerned about the situation. But all I could do was reassure her they were thinking along the right lines. Later I wondered if they'd ever get round to it in time.

POA

In WI, there is a Uniform Power of Attorney for Finances and Property, which delegates a POA for the Principle. WI statute 244 states it's "effective when executed unless the principal provides in the power of attorney that it becomes effective at a future date or upon the occurrence of a future event or contingency." An

Chapter Four – Advance Planning: General

estate-planning lawyer should be consulted to set up a POA for finances and property.

WI statute 155 deals with Health Care POA, which is different from POA for Finances and Property. A POA for finances can, for example, write checks for the Principle if the written document provides for that (which is why a lawyer should be consulted). POA for healthcare, on the other hand, invokes the following language: "I understand that.... (name of principal) has designated me to be his or her health care agent or alternate health care agent *if he or she is ever found to have incapacity and unable to make health care decisions himself or herself* (emphasis added). (Name of principal) has discussed his or her desires regarding health care decisions with me."

Therefore, for a healthcare POA to be able to make decisions on behalf of the Principle, the Principle first needs to be "adjudicated incompetent." WI statute 155.05 states: "Unless otherwise specified in the power of attorney for health care instrument, an individual's power of attorney for health care takes effect upon a finding of

Chapter Four – Advance Planning: General

incapacity by 2 physicians, as defined in s. 448.01 (5), or one physician and one licensed advanced practice clinician, who personally examine the principal and sign a statement specifying that the principal has incapacity. Mere old age, eccentricity or physical disability, either singly or together, are insufficient to make a finding of incapacity. Neither of the individuals who make a finding of incapacity may be a relative of the principal or have knowledge that he or she is entitled to or has a claim on any portion of the principal's estate. A copy of the statement, if made, shall be appended to the power of attorney for health care instrument." This makes it evident that an estate-planning lawyer should be consulted.

What all this means is that if there is a *healthcare* POA document and it's not activated yet, the POA cannot make any decisions on behalf of the Principle. Often in the ER, someone would come in and say they were the POA (for healthcare), but we always asked if it had been activated. Many times it had not. If the senior's living situation is such that it's necessary to activate the POA, it's

Chapter Four – Advance Planning: General

best not to wait until there is a crisis. Because the procedure understandably takes time.

Guardians

" 'Guardian' means a person appointed by a court under s. 54.10 to manage the income and assets and provide for the essential requirements for health and safety and the personal needs of an individual found incompetent…" (WI Statute 54) Guardians can be relatives or someone the court selects. A spouse could be a guardian for the other, or parents could be guardians for disabled adult children. They can designate who will succeed them. It should be established ahead of time who will be responsible for the disabled party, so that a sudden medical event affecting the caregiver (parent) doesn't cause a court appointment (of a guardian) to become necessary.

Estate planning

Whether or not your parents are ready to make a move, estate planning is a must. In fact, if you haven't

Chapter Four – Advance Planning: General

done it yourself, *now* is the time to take action! Here are a few facts regarding estate planning:

- Having a will doesn't prevent an estate having to go through probate
- If a will was made prior to a remarriage, consult a lawyer regarding because WI is a marital property state (the lawyer will be able to explain)
- Setting up a trust can enable probate avoidance (ask the lawyer)
- Not everything passes through probate; for example, beneficiary accounts, POD (payable on death) or TOD (transfer on death). Ask an estate-planning lawyer if TOD for a home is advisable: sometimes it's *not*. Make sure the beneficiaries for accounts and insurance policies are updated!
- Update all accounts and the will whenever there is a change, or even after a lapse of years, to ensure they reflect current wishes
- Using an estate-planning lawyer is a must whenever there is a more complicated estate and highly recommended all the rest of the time

Chapter Four – Advance Planning: General

- Trying to use WI real estate laws regarding ownership to do DIY estate-planning can be disastrous
- Part of estate planning could be taking out a long-term care insurance policy

> Betty, an elderly widow, bought a second home for cash and put her eldest son Tom on the deed as a joint tenant with rights of survivorship. The assumption was that she would predecease him and then he would sell it and divide the funds equally with his siblings. They thought they were smart to "save money" by not paying an estate-planning lawyer.
>
> One the way home from the title company, they were in a terrible crash. Betty died instantly, but Tom lingered long enough to inherit the estate. Then he eventually died intestate. He had no kids. His estranged wife (they were planning a divorce) inherited the house. If Betty had survived Tom and died intestate, all four of her kids would have inherited it. Her intentions were not carried out because she didn't consult an estate planning lawyer.

Chapter Four – Advance Planning: General

Perhaps you and/or your parents have already consulted an estate-planning lawyer and feel well-prepared. It still is a good idea to ask your parents when they last updated their will...and *if they also updated their POD/TOD documents* at the same time. Sometimes people update their wills and trusts, but forget about policies that may have unwanted beneficiaries (like an ex-spouse or pre-deceased heir) listed. Or they may forget about the policy altogether. POD and TOD assets do not go through probate, so keeping all documents related to estate planning in one place makes it easier to keep these updated.

Chapter Four – Advance Planning: General

> Mary and Jack had several investments, including numerous beneficiary accounts. Some of these were not jointly held: Mary had accounts that she held separately from Jack. Jack died, and she set up new beneficiaries for policies and accounts because he was no longer the beneficiary.
>
> Unfortunately, she forgot one account, a life insurance annuity. Four years later, Mary died and her PR disbursed everything according to her will, which had been written *before* the policy existed. Nobody knew about it. Two years after that, the insurance company managed to track down the PR and asked the whereabouts of Jack "because he was the beneficiary." The PR had to provide documentation proving Jack's prior death among other things.

Advance planning may seem out of place in a book about transitioning from one living arrangement to the next, but it's actually vital. It would make no sense for a couple to move from a 5-bed 2-story to a condo because

Chapter Four – Advance Planning: General

of health issues and then still have no plan for what happens when the more able one becomes disabled.

Or when one of them is demonstrably unfit to make decisions anymore, and the other one needs to manage the finances but can't because there are no joint accounts. *Merely* making a move may help with some situations (such as driving), but won't have any impact on other aspects, such as financial, unless planning has taken place.

Chapter Four – Advance Planning: General

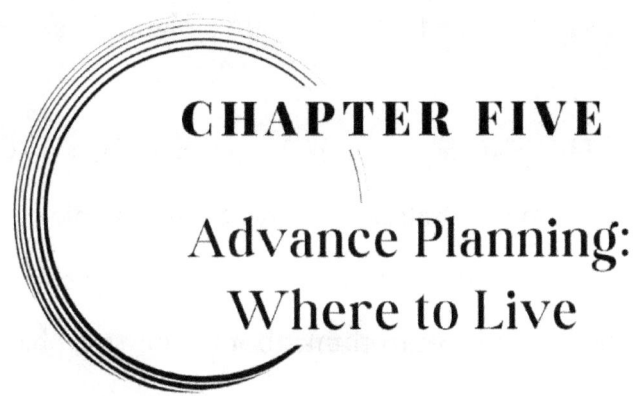

CHAPTER FIVE

Advance Planning: Where to Live

Looking ahead to future housing options can be considered a form of advance planning, even if it's not exactly a legal process. Your senior parents may be equipped to stay at home for an indefinite period, but it still is wise to make advance plans in the context of housing. These plans should include choices of where they would like to live if it becomes literally impossible to stay at home. They may already have designated POAs and a PR for their estate, written a will, created a trust, or investigated alternative living situations…or they may have

Chapter Five – Advance Planning: Where to Live

done *none* of those things! Advance planning encompasses all of these.

The first step is to find out what plans they have made, if you don't already know. Some people procrastinate even making wills, because it's something they just don't want to think about. They may have to go through the *stages of decision-making* simply to do that. Possibly the best way to get started with advance planning is to have a family discussion.

Planning (with family dynamics)

"I've been older since before you were born." "Stop *looking* at me!" "I'll *tell!*" Can you relate to any of these? If you have at least one sibling, you can probably recall hearing or saying things like this. It's funny…until it isn't. Jane Mersky Leder said, "Our siblings push buttons that cast us in roles we felt sure we had let go of long ago."

This becomes painfully apparent when there is a major life transition involving parents. In ER, it was all too common to have the adult children of an elderly patient arguing about the best course to take, or even accusing one

Chapter Five – Advance Planning: Where to Live

another. All this would be precipitated by the strong emotions that surfaced due to the emergency situation.

Knowing that this can occur will help all parties to prepare mentally ahead of time, but it takes a conscious effort. One way to prepare *mentally* is to prepare *practically* when there is no emergent situation. Then if there is any sudden change, everyone can take a deep breath and remember, "We discussed this all ahead of time."

In any sibling group people fall into different roles. Person A might be the one to plan a surprise party, for example, or do research on choosing a professional to work with. Person B might be the one who says, "Give me a list and I'll get it done." Person C might be the one who soothes ruffled feelings among the others. Person D might say, "Whatever you guys decide, that's fine. I'll send money, but don't expect me to plan." If you have siblings, you know what I mean.

In helping your parents make decisions about transitioning from one place to another, it pays to make sure everyone is communicating effectively. This is crucial when some live out of town and some are daily interacting

Chapter Five – Advance Planning: Where to Live

with the parents. They will have different perspectives almost automatically.

It's all too common for the children that see their parents daily or weekly to be unaware of a decline. Then when their sister from Wyoming flies in, she's shocked at the changes she sees, and starts pressing, "We have to *do* something!" The at-home siblings might respond, "They're doing really well for their age" to which Sis might say, "Most people their age are *dead!*"

Or the hands-on, at-home kids might keep telling their far away siblings that things aren't going so well for Dad, but the ones that live in Oregon keep stating they don't know what the fuss is about because they Facetime every week and he doesn't seem too bad to them. The hands-on siblings can feel dumped on and resentment can start smoldering.

If there are differences of opinions like this it's always wise to try to see things from the other side. It's even better to try to avoid hard feelings by not waiting until a change becomes absolutely necessary. One solution is to have a *Family Discussion* about the issue at hand.

Chapter Five – Advance Planning: Where to Live

Planning a discussion

When everyone is prepared, the discussion is more likely to go well. Therefore talk to all involved and ask what their specific concerns are that they want to address. There might be out of town relatives that can't make a physical meeting but may still have something to express; get their input even if they can't be there. Then make an outline of what will be discussed, so people don't get sidetracked into reminiscing, gossiping, arguments about events long past, or other issues that will detract from the issue/s at hand.

Schedule a time when people will not feel rushed and when nobody will be hungry. At that time, gather everyone possible, and literally sit in a circle, which always helps facilitate open discussions. Then each takes a turn talking about the issues and concerns listed on the outline, while one person can take notes. The out-of-town people can Facetime, Zoom, or call in. Or just send an email listing their concerns.

The theme of the discussion will be determined by the topics. It could be a siblings-only primary meeting with

Chapter Five – Advance Planning: Where to Live

a secondary one including the parents to follow. It could be simply talking over distributing a collection, or it could involve actually making a move. It could be centered around "Which place?" or "How can we help them stay safely where they are?" or "How do we distribute all that stuff so they can move/stay?"

The family discussion should involve the senior parents if it involves any aspect of estate planning. For example, if they haven't made or updated a will, this is the time to tell them about your worries. Will they need a trust? Do they want to try probate avoidance? If there is no will, no POAs, or no PR for the estate, the talk **needs** to include getting an estate-planning lawyer to help with that. Otherwise, the estate will be disbursed according to WI law no matter the decedent's preferences. It will be worth the lawyer's fee to have that settled!

Advance planning for making a move

Unlike estate planning, advance planning for making a move is a little more low-key. This involves gathering information on all available housing options, then making

Chapter Five – Advance Planning: Where to Live

an *advance decision* as to where your parents might choose to live if a sudden medical event means they must move sooner than planned.

Discussing advance housing plans with your parents should not seem nearly as threatening to them as a "you need to move now" type of discussion. And it can open the way to start them thinking about actually making a transition before being forced to. Ask them if they might feel more comfortable in a ranch home instead of in a two-story. Or a condo instead of a place where they have to do maintenance. (Sometimes it's possible just to pay someone to do the yardwork, though, instead of buying a condo).

Offer to research different alternative housing possibilities. These would be places to rent instead of buy. These alternatives make sense especially if there are progressive health issues that will require increasing levels of care. If someone can move into a RCAC straightaway instead of trading a Colonial for a ranch, and *then* having to move *again*…well, why not go straight for the RCAC?

Chapter Five – Advance Planning: Where to Live

Housing options

There is a variety of options for seniors to choose from In considering each, the health and safety (present and projected) of the individuals should be accounted for. Options include:

- Income based. Open to anybody who meets the (low) income requirements
- Senior condos (rented)
- Senior apartments, income-based or not income-based
- Assisted living

We'll explore each type below.

Income-based

If you are facing a low-income situation, besides opportunities for senior housing, there is Section 8. One couple that was finding remaining in their home too difficult financially were able to sell and rent from a Section 8 landlord. If the idea of a larger complex doesn't appeal to your parents, you can see about getting them on

Chapter Five – Advance Planning: Where to Live

a Section 8 housing list as my clients did. There may be a landlord that will rent to them.

Senior Condos

There are some places that have condos to rent, not buy. These condos are for those who want truly independent living. Some facilities may allow the condo tenants to eat at the main campus if they also incorporate an RCAC at that site. If medical needs change, a person can move from the condo into the apartment for greater levels of care and remain on the same campus.

Senior apartments, either income- or not income-based

There are different types of these. Some are high-rise and some are *cottage style*; almost like a ground level string of condos. These are for seniors who are independent, and they don't offer meals. They are "zero-entry"-no steps to get into them-and usually have attached garages.

Chapter Five – Advance Planning: Where to Live

Sometimes the managers organize field trips, and often the residents themselves plan get-togethers: groups for sewing, card playing, or potlucks. Staying in a place like this is much safer than staying in a single-family home. Because the neighbors tend to look out for each other and quickly notice if someone isn't following their usual routine.

Assisted Living

Assisted living refers to three types of facilities: Residential Care Apartment Complex (RCAC), Community Based Residential Facility (CBRF), and Adult Family Home (AFH). WI statutes relating to them can be found at

https://docs.legis.wisconsin.gov/code/admin_code/dhs/030/89

https://docs.legis.wisconsin.gov/code/admin_code/dhs/030/83/_1

https://docs.legis.wisconsin.gov/code/admin_code/dhs/030/88

Chapter Five – Advance Planning: Where to Live

RCAC

RCACs serve those who want to maintain independence but also have the security of onsite staff, and the option to have meals onsite. They can be Certified or Registered. Certified RCACs can take both private pay and Medicaid-eligible residents ("...shall comply with all other applicable requirements of the Medicaid Community Waivers Manual" WI DHS 89.52)

Registered RCACs may be inspected at any time by DHS, but they are not *routinely* inspected. They are not required to have a contract with the county agency that administers the medical assistance waiver.

All RCACs are required to have full kitchens, private bathrooms, living, and sleeping areas in the apartments. They must have their own private entrance and exit, and are to be physically separated from any CBRF or nursing home that may also be on the campus.

There will be a comprehensive assessment prior to being admitted, which will include physical, nutritional, mental/emotional, behavioral/social, and monitoring needs. The RCAC will then develop a service agreement in

Chapter Five – Advance Planning: Where to Live

collaboration with the tenant, which must include details about services, fees, and policies and procedures. The service agreement may be updated at the request of the tenant or facility, or when there is a change in the comprehensive assessment.

For a list of RCACs, you may refer to the information provided by your County's ADRC or go to https://www.dhs.wisconsin.gov/guide/rcacdir.pdf

CBRF

CBRFs have a higher level of care than RCACs. For example, RCACs are not allowed to have tenants with an activated POA for Healthcare, but CBRFs are allowed. RCACs cannot have residents with court-appointed guardians, but CBRFs can.

CBRFs require an initial assessment similar to that for RCACs, and there are different classes of CRBFs: A, AS, ANA, CA, CS, and CNA. They are licensed according to size: small, medium, and large. Who may stay in them is governed by what class they are.

Chapter Five – Advance Planning: Where to Live

A CRBF is a different arrangement than a RCAC. CRBFs provide a higher level of care than RCACs. Normally a resident in a CBRF has a room with an en suite bathroom, but no kitchen as in RCACs. Meals are taken in the dining room, and there are common areas like large living rooms, where people can congregate. There are no options for residents to cook in a CBRF, but most folks do have a small apartment size refrigerator.

Residents can be responsible for taking any medication they have, but in reality, most residents in CBRFs are given their medications, instead of self-taking them. CBRFs are required to monitor residents' health and maintain medical records.

For a list of CBRFs, you may refer to information provided by your County's ADRC or go to https://www.dhs.wisconsin.gov/guide/cbrfdir.pdf

AFH

AFHs are also known as *group homes* and are listed according to the population they serve. Many of them are not specifically for seniors, but there are some that cater to

Chapter Five – Advance Planning: Where to Live

"advanced age." According to DHS 88, an AFH is "...a place where 3 or 4 adults not related to the licensee reside..." Some of them take public funding.

Many other requirements are similar to RCACs and CBRFs. AFHs can allow pets. For a list of AFHs, you may refer to information provided by your County's ADRC or go to https://www.dhs.wisconsin.gov/guide/afhdir.pdf

Narrow down the choices

Once you or your parents have researched, narrow the options down to a list of places they'd actually consider. Then visit them in person. Remember, at this point, it's simply a fact-finding mission. It's just planning ahead.

After the visits, some of the places may get eliminated. Some may have average waiting lists that are just too long, if the older person knows they have to move pretty soon. (If there's one place that everyone absolutely loves, and there *is* a really long waiting list, it might pay to get on it at this point).

Chapter Five – Advance Planning: Where to Live

Now you'll have a condensed list of preferred places, and won't be caught unprepared in the event there is a sudden medical change that necessitates moving quickly. Because no *immediate* decisions need to be made at the time you're doing research, there should be no feelings of being pressured.

It's a good idea to have everyone sign this *future-home plan* so that in the event someone becomes incapacitated or everyone just forgets, there will be no arguments about places where the senior could move. You could even have this plan notarized or involve a lawyer if everyone felt it necessary.

NOTE: When the time does come to make a move, call the office of the place to make sure the ownership and management haven't changed. If there are significant unwelcome changes, move to the next one on the list.

Chapter Five – Advance Planning: Where to Live

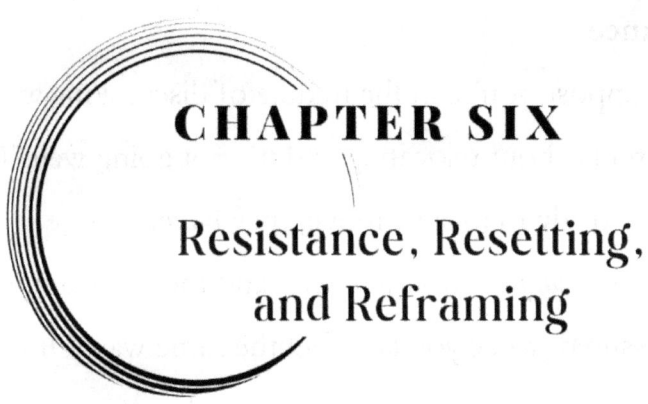

CHAPTER SIX

Resistance, Resetting, and Reframing

We encounter resistance in ourselves and others on a daily basis. Can you relate to the following? "I'm trying to lose weight" while at the same time wanting to eat a doughnut. Or "Have you finished that report yet?" while the person who is working on it is feeling pressured. Or "It'd be nice to go on vacation" while realizing there aren't the funds to do so. Resistance is (or can be) experienced in each of these examples, and resetting and reframing can help in each.

Chapter Six – Resistance, Resetting, and Reframing

Resistance

Suppose you're in the middle of discussions with your parents about relocating and it's not going well. They don't feel ready to make a move, they haven't gone through the *stages of decision-making,* and they feel anxious and pressured, while you also feel the same way. Or suppose each time you try to hint at making a move, your elderly relations shut down any attempts at conversation. They keep stonewalling and you get frustrated.

Nothing can be gained by spiraling into mutual resistance. If there is emotional gridlock that's lasting more than a few days, it might be a good idea to consider outside resources, available through the County ADRC. Having a professional evaluation of home safety helps everyone understand what needs to be done to make the current place safer, even if this might only work for a short time. It will buy everyone time.

Resetting

In the heat of a situation, it helps to step back and *reset.* Some ways to reset can be to do something fun

Chapter Six – Resistance, Resetting, and Reframing

together, like reminisce, play cards, go for a walk, watch a movie, or go out to eat. There's even a technique called 4 by 4 that can help everyone feel calmer. (It's also useful throughout the day to help you refocus at work).

You breathe in through your nose for a count of four, using your diaphragm, not your chest. Hold for four, then breathe out through pursed lips for four. Wait for another count of four before breathing in again. Repeat three times. (There are variations of this found online).

Resetting is helpful to restore clear thinking. After resetting comes reframing, which is useful in many situations. You may hear motivational speakers using the term.

Reframing

This concept involves training the thought process to look at a situation a different way. For example, someone who's hired for a junior management position might find herself being told to clean out and organize cubicles on her first day. She can look at the situation resentfully and threaten to quit, or she can tell herself,

Chapter Six – Resistance, Resetting, and Reframing

"I'll do this so they will trust me and give me better work to do in the future."

Or someone has been given a task he is dreading. His initial focus is fear. If the goal is ultimately to help someone else, he can reframe the situation as, "I'm here to help these people. It means a lot to me to be able to help by _____."

Versions of this concept are seen in the following common statements:

- I'll do ____ so that _____
- Every no is a step toward yes
- The work itself is the reward
- If not this, then something better
- "Whether you think you can, or whether you think you can't…you're right!"

These are not all true all the time but they are *truisms*. The mind has more power than we give it credit for. The *Journal of Physical Education and Sport* had an article on how mindset exercises helped basketball players improve their free throws. "…When female basketball athletes master the physical techniques *and mental training*

Chapter Six – Resistance, Resetting, and Reframing

(italics mine) provided, then it is the mental strength that will bring them to their best performance…" (JPES), Vol. 24 (issue 6), Art 161 https://efsupit.ro/images/stories/june2024/Art%20161.pdf

The point of reframing

So…how does reframing help when it's time to consider resizing? Think of the unspoken communication first. For instance, your mom keeps saying "It's overwhelming" and you've determined that what she means is feeling unable to cope with sorting through mountains of accumulations. Reframing might sound like, "Here's a joke: How do you eat an elephant? One bite at a time. All we have to do are *these* boxes. We can leave everything else for later; we'll just eat *that* bite. And then you won't have so much to do later."

What if your dad says he just knows he'll hate living in X? He will be focusing on something negative. Reframe it to ask the question, "You mean you'll hate living closer to us?" In that scenario, he could be encouraged to say,

Chapter Six – Resistance, Resetting, and Reframing

"I'll move so that I can see my family more often." Or just ask what he might find to like about the plan. The lists of pros and cons mentioned in Chapter 1 will reveal at least *some* pros; get him to focus on those.

Some parents have worries that by selling their house to rent a condo or apartment, they'll use up their kids' inheritance. Obviously, this will need to be explored at the family discussion. It may be a valid concern.

But very often, children of elderly parents don't care about or need more money. *Their* concerns are parents having a more convenient place to live, or increased safety by having assistance at hand in case of falls. Reframing in that situation can sound like, "We are really looking forward to having you stay in a better (safer) place" instead of focusing on the money issue that worries them. Try to get them to focus on, "If I do X, then I'll make my kids happy" rather than "This is all I have to leave to them." And proper estate planning can lessen the risk of "losing money."

Reframing could be helpful if there is home maintenance that isn't being done (or done well). Instead

Chapter Six – Resistance, Resetting, and Reframing

of having the thought of "This is my home; I just won't leave," your elderly relatives could be encouraged to think of all the free time they'll have if they move to a place without those maintenance chores. They'll have time to pursue hobbies, or sort through all the old photographs they've been meaning to get to. Or they won't have to worry about replacing the roof or fixing a rotten window.

If your aunt isn't eating well because she hates cooking, she could be encouraged to consider a place where all or most meals are provided. "Just think, no more cooking or dishes to do!" appeals to a lot of people. There are some places where people can rent an independent apartment or condo and opt-in to eat in the dining room of the RCAC that also happens to be on the same campus.

Brainstorming with extended family can help you both to understand the true cause of resistance, and also how to reframe into something positive. Just give it time.

Chapter Six – Resistance, Resetting, and Reframing

CHAPTER SEVEN

The Process

Once your relatives decide to resize and sell their home, there will be choices as to how to proceed. There are two basic ways to sell a property: "as-is" or with updates. Please note, "as-is" is not really a legal term, but it usually means the seller is unwilling or unable to pay for repairs.

Too often when people say they want to sell as-is, what they really mean is they want full market price without doing repairs or updating. There is a difference between full market price and as-is price!

Chapter Seven – The Process

It's important to understand that *selling as-is* means the house will *net an as-is price*.

Sell as-is	Make Some Decor Upgrades
• Assumes people will pay the same for a non-updated home: they WON'T. Most people get a "bad feeling" that makes them not like the house	• Most people cannot see past what's right in front of them. No imagination: if it looks better, they respond better
• People who are willing to do a lot of projects expect a lower price; they are looking for a *deal*	• People who are willing to pay top price, do NOT want to have to do any work or are unable to make repairs. Most are overworked, with 3 or even 4 jobs & just want to come home & relax, not do projects
• Limited buyer pool: those who have the time, inclination, and ability to fix things	• Updated decor provides the biggest possible buyer pool. Many people will not even want to see a house they find unappealing
• Price MUST reflect how it looks; decor hurts as much or even more than structural issues	• Flooring, kitchens, & bathrooms matter the most, but also the first room they see
• Evaluate the cost vs benefit. Top price cannot be obtained without updating	• People used to imagine upgrades cost more than they really do, but now, it really might be as expensive as they fear; check costs
• Some sellers only want fast sale and don't mind getting an "as-is" price	• Better price; sometimes markedly so

Chapter Seven – The Process

Evaluate the commitment: is it to Price or is it to Selling? If Price, then the house has to be "worth it" to people. Even if updated, they won't make offers if they think it's too high. *Don't* use the home to sell the competition's houses!

32% of my business now comes from people that tried to sell in the past, but couldn't:

- Case 1: Tried 4 times to sell; had a "designer" color that no other agent told them was the problem. They thought they had to install marble countertops, but all they needed was paint. Under contract in 5 days, because they did what I advised
- Case 2: Tried 1 time to sell; had a yellow kitchen. Sold after following my advice.
- Case 3: Tried to sell 3 times; had wallpaper in kitchen & baths. Nobody had told them to get rid of it. Removed the paper after being advised to do so. Under contract in 5 days.

The market ALWAYS talks: if nobody comes to see it, they are "screaming" that they don't like it.

Chapter Seven – The Process

Beware Google reviews

Many people look up professionals on Google or other platforms. But don't reject an agent just because they aren't found there. Some agents will not have a big online presence, but that is not an indicator of their skill level. And (per my broker) there are ways to fake reviews, either for good or bad. So if someone doesn't appear in a search, or has no reviews, maybe they simply didn't want to get involved in online drama.

You might wish to consider agents that have experience in dealing with seniors or that have additional credentials. If so, you'd need to have that as one of your questions when you interview them. Because it is indeed imperative to *speak* to the agents, instead of just stalking them on the internet!

Interviewing agents in person helps you determine if the agent you speak to is someone you want to hire. That will give the agent and you a chance to communicate in a way that's not possible merely through email or text, because at least half of communication is body language.

Chapter Seven – The Process

That plus tone of voice, adds up to about 90%. Therefore face-to-face is the best form of communication.

Even if you live in another state, it's still better to have a phone call followed by email, than to rely merely on texts or emails. Sometimes Zoom or FB can be used.

Beware pricing unsupported by data

Home sellers can make the mistake of asking their children who live in other states (or even locally) for advice as to pricing, instead of relying on the professional agent or appraiser they hired. I recall one seller with a daughter in CA and one in NYC who asked their input as to a good starting price. Of course, WI prices are nowhere near the prices in those places! The best practice is to get professional opinions, either from agents or an appraiser.

To start with, family members might have an emotional tie which can color their thinking. One time, a relative of a seller suggested a price that was 35% above known appraised value! Obviously, if the house were listed at that price, it wouldn't sell. Even supposing it got an inflated offer that matched the price, it's doubtful that the

Chapter Seven – The Process

new appraisal (from the buyer's bank) would be much different than the old one. And homes *have* to appraise so the buyer can get the loan.

At times, parents' decisions to re-size are complicated by a "committee" with siblings, children, nieces, nephews, grandkids all wanting to chime in. This is understandably intricate. When so many people want to have a say in what happens, it can become difficult to make any decisions at all.

I have been in these situations, and what seems to work best is to have a round table discussion (literally everyone sitting in a circle), where everyone is asked to express themselves: the Family Discussion previously mentioned. Take notes; it helps. Please remember, though, that the final decision belongs to the people that actually own the house.

Please resist the temptation to tell your relatives what to ask for their house, especially if this varies a lot from values suggested by a comparative market analysis (CMA), or if you live out-of-town. You certainly can get more than one analysis if you need to compare. Or you might even

Chapter Seven – The Process

get an actual appraisal done by a licensed appraiser. Appraisals are considered the final word when it comes to market value, but you do have to pay for them.

Consider the fact that all decisions need to be based on data, so an agent should be able to show and explain the data. The best CMAs use the most data points. You should also be given data on the current competition, which is a separate data set in my opinion. Because homes that are *listed* for a price, may *sell* for a different price, either more or less.

The purpose of understanding the competition is so that your price doesn't help sell someone else's house. Because buyers are always looking at the competition and comparing! Remember that an appraisal is highly recommended in any situation where multiple people just cannot agree on a price: then at least there will be an expert's input to go by.

Beware of not having the house ready

If there's time to prepare before calling an agent, you or your parents may already have packed or removed

Chapter Seven – The Process

many items from the house. Even so, there might still be more decluttering and/or staging to do. Each house is different, but generally a home should look "lived in but not *too* lived in."

Staging doesn't always mean having to hire a professional stager to come in and redo the house. Only my high-end listings used a professional stager. Often it can be as simple as removing knick knacks or photos, or moving a piece of furniture. An experienced agent will be able to make suggestions. Resisting these suggestions has the potential to make the house less show-worthy, so please consider them carefully.

At times there can be bigger projects to do, such as painting or repairs. Everyone will have to plan how to get these things finished. Sometimes it's best for the homeowners to move out first. If that's not possible, see if a contractor can come in and get it done quickly, if it's something simple like painting.

Some repairs, like a roof or septic system, can be done even after closing if needed, by escrowing for them. Believe it or not, they are less likely to affect sellability than

Chapter Seven – The Process

cosmetic issues, as long as buyers are informed in the MLS that these repairs will need to be done and that sellers will escrow for them.

Beware long DOM

DOM (days on market) is the length of time a property sits before getting an offer. The average DOM will reflect how fast houses are selling and indicate if it's a buyers' market (long DOM) or seller's market. Whatever the average DOM is for the price bracket, is how long you can expect the house to be without offers.

For example, in a buyer's market, the average DOM could be 212 days. As long as your listing has not been on the market longer than the average, you don't really have to worry. On the other hand in a seller's market, it's common for houses to get offers within the first 5 days or even the first few hours if the market is super-hot.

DOM is important, because you *do not want it to be over the average.* Any time a house sits on the market, it becomes "shopworn" and buyers automatically believe

Chapter Seven – The Process

there "must be something wrong with it." Even if there's nothing "wrong" but the price!

If you have committed to Price (vs Selling), expect your listing to be on the market longer than average. (The seasons can also play a part in this). It's possible it could still sell, but understand that-depending on how high the price is-it may not sell at all.

Or it will sell for less than what it could have, if it'd been listed at a competitive price to begin with. Every agent has seen this phenomenon! It's best to avoid this scenario by using the data to guide your decisions.

CHAPTER EIGHT

Selling the House

If the house is priced competitively, expect multiple offers in a seller's market. This is because "everyone wants to buy the house that someone else is after too." Depending on how hot the market is, there could be two or eight...or even more.

Getting offers right away, or over asking, *does not* mean it's priced too low! On the contrary, getting an offer fast indicates that the price was competitive enough to attract a buyer or buyers ready to go. There is a saying, rooted in reality, that "Homes that sell fast, sell for top dollar." Offers written in a seller's market will strongly

Chapter Eight – Selling the House

favor the sellers, because multiple buyers are crawling over each other to get the house.

At times sellers become ambitious when it's a seller's market and decide to list at the top of the range of potential price points. It's never wise to do this in a neutral or buyer's market, but sellers can get away with it if the market is hot. What I've seen is that these listings do take longer to get offers, but still may sell for full price. Usually there is only one offer, and it's almost never over asking.

In a buyer's market, the seller may have to wait quite a while to get an offer because there are so many houses for buyers to choose from. Offers in a buyer's market will have terms that strongly favor the buyers, because if they don't get what they want, they'll just choose another property.

Should people take the first offer that comes along? Statistically speaking, yes. This is because there is a *buying cycle*. What this means is that buyers will typically view between eight to twelve houses before deciding to make an offer. (Keeping the buying cycle in mind, that also means

Chapter Eight – Selling the House

there will statistically be eight to twelve showings before getting an offer).

Therefore, if a buyer is making an offer, they've *already been through the cycle* and are serious about buying. So the first offer is often the best one; this is a well-known truism. That first offer should not necessarily be ignored even if it's not what was expected. Because that buyer is serious! When there are multiple offers, the "best" one might be the third of six that come in on the same day, so the truism that the "first is best" is not to be taken literally.

> Chuck declined the first offer he got, because he wanted more money. As time went on, more people viewed the home, and he received five more offers, each successively lower, until the final offer was $45K less than the first. He ended up taking the house off the market.

Of course, there are times when the first offer is not the best. This is most likely to happen when the house has been sitting on the market for a while, and may also have had a price adjustment. A buyer who's been watching knows that the price dropped and wants to see how low they can go. In this case, often the seller will try a counter offer. It's best to avoid having to face this by *pricing competitively at the beginning*.

Responding to Offers

The response to offers is based on how many there are. In a bidding war situation, there will be more than one to choose from. Note, a bidding war does not mean that the buyers get to see one another's offers; it's more like contractors submitting sealed bids for a project.

In this scenario, people pick the best one and reject the others. What constitutes "best" isn't always the price. Variables include terms of the offer, who the lender is, and what loan type the buyer is using, plus other possibilities.

Often a home will get just one offer. Remember, one is all it takes to sell a home! It's a bad idea not to consider that offer. It might be the only one!

Chapter Eight – Selling the House

If the offer has terms that aren't acceptable, the seller can send a counter offer to the buyer, who then can accept, counter, or reject the counter. This can go on like a game of ping pong until either one party accepts a counter or decides to let the deal drop and walk away. Until a counter offer is accepted, there is no deal, so counters should be used with discretion.

Sometimes there could be multiple offers, with none standing out as especially good. In this case, a seller may decide to use a *multiple counter proposal* that gets sent to all the buyers at once. Then they have to respond to the proposal, and the seller gets the final say. This is risky because if *all* the buyers decide not to accept the multiple counters, the seller ends up with no offers at all.

Accepted Offer

Once an offer is accepted, the sellers have to pack. This is why it's best to start downsizing or packing before even listing a home: there will be less to do later on. There are actually senior moving companies that specialize

Chapter Eight – Selling the House

working for the senior population. (And don't forget to call the utility companies to arrange final readings!)

Sometimes people procrastinate downsizing or packing, and then get in a panic because they have to have all their stuff out of the house by the closing date. Some have even rented storage units. This may be a temporary solution to "too much stuff" but remember, it costs money every month. If you do end up using one, set a deadline to sort through the stored items. Otherwise, it is just a money pit.

Closing (Sale)

This is when the house is finally sold. Many people use the phrase, "we sold our house" to refer to being under contract. But remember, "It's not sold til it's sold!"

Many situations can arise which require troubleshooting by the agent. Most of them are minor, but if any major issue comes up, the agent's skill and expertise become crucial. This is why you should understand what the agent's *knowledge base* is, before they are hired: don't be afraid to ask how they troubleshoot.

Chapter Eight – Selling the House

Whatever your parents' new situation is, it's time to make the most of it. It can be common for people to become depressed or withdrawn in the first month of a new living situation, but after that, you can expect that they will be more themselves. It just takes time.

Not everyone will react that way! In fact, they may surprise you at how active they become in their new place, especially if there are scheduled happenings. Some people truly get a new lease on life, once they no longer have to worry about maintenance, repairs, and bills. I've seen it! Whatever happens, just being there and supporting them through the adjustment will be appreciated.

For all of us, tomorrow is the "first day of the rest of our lives." Having your relatives in a safe environment will help both you and them take advantage of that day and all the days that follow.

Examples taken from the HSSAT, or Home Safety Self-Assessment Tool. Acknowledgments for drawings, John A. Nyquist, MS, CMI.

Living Room

Entrance to Back/Side Door

About the Author

A native of West Allis, WI, Emily met & married "A" in the UK. They came to the US with four children and settled in WI. She earned a BSN from UW-Milwaukee, and obtained her nursing license in 1996, shortly before her fifth child was born. She currently lives outside Kiel, Wisconsin.

Her nursing background encompasses nursing home, MedSurg, surgery center, home health, and ER, in which specialty she spent 22 years. She also served as a trainer for staff at a local CBRF and worked per diem in nursing homes during her tenure in ER.

Emily has done extensive study in Real Estate beyond the requirements needed to obtain a real estate license. Areas of focus include the Military Relocation Professional and Senior Real Estate Specialist, as well as many other designations.

In late 2023, Emily became a Homes for Heroes Agent Affiliate. Homes for Heroes is a program that was developed after 9/11 by a group in MN. H4H agents donate part of their compensation to the organization, which then provides a "Hero Reward" to recipients after closing. The Hero populations include people who work or worked in Education, EMS/Fire, Healthcare, Law enforcement, and Military. And even support staff qualify! To find out more about Homes for Heroes and how it works, go to www.ishomesforheroesascam.com

Contact Information

www.linkedin.com/in/emily-matthews-re-agent
(Emily Matthews RE Agent)

www.facebook.com/EmilyMatthewsWIRealtor
(Emily Matthews RE Agent)

www.youtube.com/@EmilyMatthewsREagent
(Emily Matthews RE Agent)

www.emilymatthewsreagent.com

Phone Number: (920) 286-0570

www.ingramcontent.com/pod-product-compliance
Lightning Source LLC
Chambersburg PA
CBHW071724040426
42446CB00011B/2202